Contents

No Quick Fix

Don't be fooled by those who will tell you that you can raise your score by hundreds of points in a few days with some magic formula.

It's really up to you how fast your score increases. You have to know what's on your report, dispute the negative info and pay down high balances.

There are a few other things you can do like becoming an authorized user on someone else's card. You can contact lenders and dispute late payments.

This book is written to give you the facts about your report and score without all the hype.

What Is In My Credit Report?

Most people are aware of what their credit report contains. If you are not sure or need to refresh your memory, read on.

Information about you and your past credit history; how much you owe, whether you pay on time or have had any late payments or unfavorable accounts will be recorded in your credit file.

Collections or public records such as bankruptcies or foreclosures, your current and previous addresses and your employment data will be listed. The name of your employer could also be on there.

Your credit file does not have information about your bank account, education or marital status, race religion or national origin, although it may have the name of your spouse.

Account numbers, names and addresses of the companies that you owe and the dates that the item will be removed are also included. Your social security number, birth date, phone number and other different spellings of your name will also be in the file.

When you are applying for a loan, it is important to be consistent with how you spell your name, whether or not you add a middle initial, etc. because the creditor will report it to the agency as it is written.

The report contains your satisfactory and unsatisfactory accounts. Most lenders report changes in account status on a monthly basis. However, if you make a payment, it may not appear for up to 30 days. Older accounts are gradually removed.

Your report will list how many inquiries you have had. Inquiries are the number of times that lenders have looked at your report, giving them a snapshot of how often you have asked for credit.

Too many hard inquiries impact your score in a negative way. Promotional and account review inquiries have no effect. Viewing your own free report has no impact on your score.

Who Can Get Access to My Report?

There are limits to who can access your report according to the Fair Credit Reporting Act (FCRA). You are entitled to a copy of your own report without affecting your score.

Creditors, including employers, landlords and insurance companies are allowed to check your credit but they must have your permission to do so. Keep in mind that these are hard inquiries and will affect your score. Lenders, credit card companies, landlords and other sources report your information to three major agencies in the United States. These three are: Transunion, Experian and Equifax.

Your report is then compiled based on what they have reported. Not all lenders report to all bureaus so your information may differ from one bureau to another depending on what has been reported. This can result in 3 different scores. Some lenders will request copies from all three reporting agencies and typically use the middle score.

Creditors will check your report when you apply for any type of loan. If you buy a car, get a credit card or apply for a mortgage, an inquiry will be logged. The terms and the rate of interest that you will pay will be based on what is in the report and your credit score.

Remember, they must have your permission to check your credit report.

What is a Credit Score?

A score is a number given to you based on information about how you have handled your credit accounts. The higher your score is the better for you because it means that you are a lower risk for lenders that want to extend credit to you.

You may pay a lower interest rate and get more flexible terms if your score is higher. Over several years you could pay a lot more for the loan, depending on the rate and closing fees, if your score is low. You could save hundreds of dollars in interest if your score is higher. It is definitely to your advantage to keep a good score.

The Fair Isaac Corporation (FICO) uses a range of 300 to 850. They use formulas to figure your score. Your score is important in understanding how much borrowing ability that you may have.

The goal of having credit scores is to help creditors decide if you would be a risk or if you would be safe to do business with. A low score is reflective of poor management. Lenders may decide that loaning you money would be a bad risk.

You may not be able to rent a house or apartment, get utilities turned on or internet service without a security deposit if your score is low. Keeping balances low and paying off revolving accounts will help you raise your score to a higher number.

Computer programs calculate your score based on an analysis of the information found in your credit report. Payment history, use of available credit, length of time you have had credit and hard inquiries are all factors in determining your score. Lenders want to know what your risk factor is in comparison to other consumers.

If you request your score from an agency, you may have to pay for it. Some companies will give you the score free when you apply for a loan, such as a mortgage. Many card companies have started giving their customers free scores included with the account.

You are entitled to receive a copy of your report and score when you apply for a loan, whether or not you are approved. The creditor is required to give you the answer in writing and state the reason behind the decision, if you are denied.

Standards vary from one lender to another, but here is a starting point for you to consider when shopping for credit products:

Poor: 300-579, **Fair**: 580-669, **Good**: 670-739,

Very Good: 740-799

Excellent: 800-850.

Understanding the Numbers

Poor: 300 to 579

The *poor* range is considered a high risk range given to those who may have had major credit problems such as bankruptcy. You may only qualify for a secured credit card. That means you will have to have a cash deposit equal to your spending limit. You may also have to have security deposits for cable, phones and utility companies. You could be turned down for credit if your score falls within this range.

Fair: 580 to 669

You will be able to qualify for some credit products if your score is *fair*, but it could disqualify you from being approved for many loans. You will pay much higher rates and will be considered a subprime borrower. You will not be offered the best rates for credit cards and may have to get a secured credit card at first.

Good: 670 to 739

If your score falls within these numbers, you may qualify for a variety of credit cards and loans. This is a *good* score accepted by many lenders, but you may be charged slightly higher rates.

Very good: 740 to 799

You will qualify for a great many loans and better interest rates from creditors if your credit score is *very good*.

Excellent: 800 to 850

With a score in the *excellent* range, you are likely to be approved for any type of loan. You will be offered the lowest interest rates with fewer fees. You can save money on home mortgages, automobiles and get better credit card offers.

The better your score, the better offers you will receive. You will save money on rates and fees by maintaining a good to excellent score.

Higher card limits and more power to negotiate rates and fees come with better scores. Your insurance rates will be lower and you could get the best phone deals without a security deposit.

Auto, Bankcard and Mortgage Scores

In addition, there are other scores particular to the kind of loan you are looking for. These are specific to the product that you are planning to purchase: the auto score, the mortgage score and the bankcard score.

These are business explicit FICO scores modeled to the type of purchase you are trying to make. Elements from all three reporting agencies are used to calculate these scores to predict the risk involved in lending you money.

When you are shopping for an automobile, the lender will typically check your FICO Auto Score. This score is designed for the auto financing lender to assess the risk of doing business with you should you default on your car payments. A range of 250 to 900 is used to indicate whether you are a low or high risk consumer.

If you want to buy a home, the mortgage lender will use the Mortgage Score. This is a range of 300 to 850. These scores are used to determine your credit worthiness when buying a house and are required for lenders that wish to meet the Fannie Mae and Freddie Mac requirements.

The scores for obtaining a bankcard range from 250 to 900. This Bankcard Score is tailored to the credit card industry. It is used to predict your use and repayment of card debt. The scores are based on the information in your credit report and are reflective of how you choose to spend, borrow and repay.

Credit scoring models are used to find consumers that have shown that they can be responsible with credit. Derogatory accounts carry a lot of weight but some rarely include medical debt.

Your credit usage and the length of time you have had open accounts will have a bigger influence on your scores.

.

What Can I Do To Increase My Score?

Some lenders take other things besides your credit score into consideration when making a decision on whether or not to loan you money.

Income, savings accounts, child support payments or alimony and length of employment do not affect your score but may be a factor in making the decision to approve your application for credit. Lenders may look at those things even if your score is somewhat low.

So what should you work on to increase your score? The most important is, of course, *on time* payments. Your history of paying on time has the biggest influence in calculating your credit score.

Derogatory accounts such as bankruptcy, foreclosures and accounts that have been handed over to collection agencies will bring down your score. These accounts can stay in your file for long periods of time, but will eventually be less of an influence over time.

Be sure that these accounts belong to you. If you find that your credit file is not accurate, you can dispute the information. It has to be removed if this is the case.

Your total debt and length of credit history is important. A good payment record over a substantial amount of time has a high impact on your score.

Accounts that use only 30 to 50 percent of their limit are more favorable to obtaining a higher score. This is known as your *credit utilization rate*. The number of times that you have applied for credit recently is also used in the calculation.

When you apply for credit and your file is checked it is logged as a *hard inquiry*. Too many hard inquiries have a negative effect.

If you have a low score, don't take it too personally. It does not mean that you are not a good person. Lenders are just looking for someone that they believe will be responsible enough to pay back the loan.

As you pay all your payments on time and avoid going over your spending limits, your score will increase over time. If you are careful and don't give up, you will see it improve steadily. Before long you will be in the *excellent* range.

Improve your score by spending less and paying on time. Your utilization rate is a factor. Try to keep your balance at 30 to 50 % of your total limit. 10 % is the ideal goal if you want to maintain a higher score.

Late payments remain on your report for years and have a negative impact on your score.

If you max out your card and make only minimum payments, you will pay more interest. It will take longer for your score to increase.

There is no magic way to rebuild a good history and score. It takes persistence, patience and determination. But it pays off in the long run. You get better rates, better offers and the security of knowing that credit is there when you need it.

.

What if I Don't Have a Credit History?

There are some options when you're just starting out. Secured cards are a good way to start. You make a deposit as collateral for the spending limit. Make purchases; pay regularly and on time to build a positive credit file.

You will have to pay interest if you don't pay the balance in full every month, but a secured card is only a starting option. After a few months of responsible credit management, the card company will likely increase your limit.

An annual fee is required by some companies. Make sure the account is reported to the major agencies. A positive credit history won't happen instantly, but it will happen if you are persistent and don't give up.

How Do I Get a Credit Card?

Secured cards are a good option to start with. This is a card that you open by making a cash deposit equal to the card limit. The money stays in the account as collateral. Apply for cards that offer a lower spending limit at first. You may have to pay an annual fee, but over a few months your spending limit will usually be increased if you pay on time.

Become an authorized user on a parent or another person's account. This account will show up on your credit report. Make sure it is someone that is responsible and pays bills on time. You won't be responsible for the account, but both the positive and negative information will be shown on your report.

You may want to try for store cards first. Some of these are a little easier to get.

Recovering From Bankruptcy

It's not easy to restore your good credit standing after filing bankruptcy. You need a plan that includes tough determination and patience. You need to budget wisely, build a savings account, and always pay your bills on time.

If you are determined and don't quit, you will see it gradually begin to improve. A lot depends on how you learn to curb your spending and develop your good money management skills. Your financial goals depend on it.

A new credit card is a good way to start to build your good credit standing again. Lenders can see that you are paying on time and keeping your balances low. It may be easier than you think to get a low limit card for starters and see your limit increase as you pay on time.

Some card companies will eventually offer you an unsecured card, if you show that you are responsible enough to pay on time. Different rules apply to different lenders, so know what to expect up front. Be sure to get a card from a company or bank that reports to all three bureaus.

Credit card companies know that you can only file for bankruptcy once every eight years, so their risk is minimal. That makes some of them eager to extend credit to you. Be sure to know what the deal is. Know what the rates and fees are and what you are getting into before you accept any new card offers.

You can pay the minimum payment or the balance in full every month, if you want to avoid paying interest.

Don't go overboard by getting too many cards at once. Be sure that you can handle the temptation to overspend. Bankruptcy Chapter 7 will stay on your report for 10 years. Chapter 13 stays on for 7 years.

Sometimes it is the only option you have. You can recover, but it is a slow process. You will have to pay higher rates to some lenders. However, if you can go slow and pay on time, you can rebuild your good credit standing and credit score.

Divorce and Credit

One of the hardest things you'll face in life can be the end of a marriage. The effects of a divorce on your credit report are dependent on whether or not you have joint accounts or separate accounts.

If you have joint accounts, there are some problems that you will have to work through. If you have had separate accounts there will not be much of an impact on these. The actual filing will not affect your report.

Understand the decree: If your name is on the account, the missed payments will be listed on your report. You are not off the hook, even if your spouse has been declared to be the responsible party.

If you are a cosigner or authorized user on your spouse account, contact the financial institution and ask them about your options. You may be able to convert the account to your spouse, depending on the lender.

Your credit limit may decrease due to loss of dual income. Know your decree and take steps to protect yourself.

Errors

If you find errors on your credit report notify the bureau immediately. Send a letter of dispute stating the error, the reason why you are disputing it and copies of any receipts if applicable.

If an account is old and the creditor is no longer in business you can ask them to verify the account. If no one verifies, it will be removed. If you are denied credit, the lender must give you the name and address of the agency that reported it and explain why you were denied.

You can get a free report for up to 60 days of the denial. Contact each creditor to change addresses and update personal information. Send a dispute letter to the agency if there is an error in reporting an account.

There is no quick fix if the information is correct, so beware of companies that say they will repair it for a fee. Don't get scammed!

Scams

There are counseling agencies that are legitimate, but there are quite a few that are not. It's up to you to learn which ones are really going to help you and which ones are after your hard earned money.

Don't be tempted to go for a quick easy fix only to find out in the long run that you have been had. Some indications of a crook will be asking for money up front.

Some may also advise you not to contact the agencies or tell you to give false information. They will probably not tell you of your legal rights either.

It is a federal crime to provide false information or use alternative social security numbers when trying to remove negative information from your file. Doing so may involve you in an identity theft scheme.

The first thing to do is to get your report and know what is on there. File a dispute if it is inaccurate. The data must be removed if confirmed to be incorrect.

.

Budget Your Money

It's not about what comes in as much as it is about what goes out. Financial success depends on good management. Make lists. List your income and your expenses. Subtract the lowest from the highest.

Hopefully, you will be subtracting your expenses from your income. If it's the other way around, you go from being in the black to being in the red. Not a good place to be. You will have to increase income or spend less.

You can find a lot of free budget templates just by doing a Google search. There is probably one in your word processing program. Find the one that is right for you, make a budget and stick with it.

Good financial planning will pay off in the long run. If you can reduce your debt, you will save money on interest and build a good credit file and score.

Are You Ready to Buy a House?

Types of Loans

A Conventional loan is one that is not insured by the federal government. Some banks will make this loan if the house or property does not meet the FHA standards. The lender has the option to approve or not. You may have to have a bigger down payment.

FHA loans have made it possible to apply for a home loan with a low credit score. You can apply if your score is 580 or above. This is a government backed loan through the Federal Housing Administration which is managed by Department of Housing and Urban Development (HUD).

Another advantage of FHA is the 3.5% down payment. The loan requires mortgage insurance, which may raise your monthly payment.

USDA loans are a government subsidized loan for low income families. They require little or no down payment. This program is for rural borrowers. It is managed by the Rural Housing Service (RHS) part of the Department of Agriculture.

Maps and income requirements are located on their website:
https://eligibility.sc.egov.usda.gov/eligibility.

If you find a home that you want to purchase, type in the address and you can see if the location qualifies for this type of loan.

VA Loans are offered to military service members and their families. There is no down payment and 100% financing to those who qualify. This program is guaranteed by the federal government.

Fixed rate or adjustable:

An Adjustable Rate mortgage loan has an interest rate that adjusts after a certain period of time. The rate stays the same for the first years of the loan, and then adjusts annually thereafter. Typically the terms will be 3/1 ARM or 5/1 ARM.

A Fixed Rate means that the rate stays the same for the life of the loan, unless you refinance.

What About 609 Letters?

A 609 letter is a letter sent to the agency asking them to validate certain items on your credit report. You can ask them to verify accounts by producing copies of original contracts or service agreements.

If they are unable to provide these, you can ask that they remove the accounts since they cannot be verified. It can result in accounts being removed.

Below is an example:

Greetings:

I am requesting information about items listed on my credit report according to Section 609 of the Fair Credit Reporting Act.

(List Account Numbers and Names)

I am asking for the original contracts and service agreements that have been signed by me. If you cannot verify the accuracy of these accounts, I am requesting that you please remove them from my file.

Sincerely,
(Your Name)
(Your Address, Date of Birth and Social Security Number)

Where Can I Get A Copy?

A free copy of your report from all three bureaus can be obtained at www.annualcreditreport.com .

You are entitled to one free report each year from the three major reporting agencies and may request it from this website.

If you are denied credit, the creditor is required to let you know in writing the reason for the denial and provide the name and address of the agency to contact for a free copy of your report.

Be sure to check for inaccuracies in your personal information as well as your credit history. Does all the information contained there belong to you or someone else? If you find any discrepancies, take the steps necessary to correct the errors.

Online: Visit AnnualCreditReport.com

By Phone: Call 1-877-322-8228. For TTY service, call 711 and ask the operator for 1-800-821-7232.

By Mail: Complete the Annual Credit Report Request Form (PDF, Download Adobe Reader) and mail it to:
Annual Credit Report Request Service
PO Box 105281
Atlanta, GA 30348-5281

Conclusion

I hope that this book has been helpful to you in learning about your credit file and how scores work. It is meant to be a starting point to head you in the right direction.

Do your homework. Your credit health and financial well-being are your responsibility.

The more you know the better off you will be.

Knowledge Really is Power

www.ingramcontent.com/pod-product-compliance
Lightning Source LLC
Chambersburg PA
CBHW031941170526
45157CB00008B/3266